GLASS STORM

The 2005 Stoughton, Wisconsin
TORNADO

By Sally and Mary Lovell

Orange Hat Publishing
www.orangehatpublishing.com - Waukesha, WI

Glass Storm: The 2005 Stoughton, Wisconsin Tornado
Copyrighted © 2019 Sally and Mary Lovell
ISBN 978-1-64538-065-8
First Edition

Glass Storm: The 2005 Stoughton, Wisconsin Tornado
by Sally and Mary Lovell

All Rights Reserved. Written permission must be secured from the publisher to use or reproduce any part of this book, except for brief quotations in critical reviews or articles.

For information, please contact:

Orange Hat Publishing
www.orangehatpublishing.com
Waukesha, WI

Cover design by Kaeley Dunteman
Edited by Christy Wopat

Photo credits: Susan Craver, Sara Lenz, Mary Lovell, Sally Lovell, Colin McDermott, Fritz Sorensen, Eric Schwanke, Nicole Schneider, *Wisconsin State Journal/The Capital Times* archive

The author has made every effort to ensure that the accuracy of the information within this book was correct at time of publication. The author does not assume and hereby disclaims any liability to any party for any loss, damage, or disruption caused by errors or omissions, whether such errors or omissions result from accident, negligence, or any other cause.

www.orangehatpublishing.com

This book is dedicated to the city of Stoughton, Wisconsin, and to Madi (1995-2007).

Thank you.

Table of Contents

Chapter 1 – Scotcheroos 1
Chapter 2 – Built From the Ground Up 6
Chapter 3 – The Phone Call 11
Chapter 4 – The Storm 16
Chapter 5 – There's No Way In 24
Chapter 6 – Glass Everywhere 30
Chapter 7 – What's Left? 40
Chapter 8 – Evacuation 44
Chapter 9 – Homeless 50
Chapter 10 – The Big, Bad Wolf 72
Chapter 11 – Is That Replaceable? 79
Chapter 12 – Here Comes the Family 88
Chapter 13 – Losses and Gains 95
Chapter 14 – New Beginnings 101
Chapter 15 – Bent, But Not Broken 106
Sally's Scotcheroo Recipe 112
Mary's Tornado Survival Kit 113
Reading Guide 114
About the Authors 117

CHAPTER 1

Scotcheroos

"Hey! Hands off those scotcheroos!" Sally scolded with a smile. Stephen looked up at her, pouting. "But, Mom! Just one?" Steve came around the corner just then. "All right, guys! We're off! The American Red Cross awaits my blood! Hop in the car!"

Sally smiled. "I'm so proud of you guys for going with your dad to donate blood," she said. "I'll have everything ready to go so when you return, we can head right to the funeral. And, Stephen, you can have a scotcheroo the moment you return. I promise."

Sally made sure the kids had their shoes on, then walked with Steve to the garage and ensured the kids were buckled into their seat belts. Steve hugged her goodbye, not even an inclination that just outside, the August heat was shaping up into something much worse. Sally, however, reminded Steve of the tornado watches—given when the weather is suitable for a tornado—and warnings—given when a tornado has been reported by radar or spotted by someone—that had been posted since the early afternoon. There had been a tornado warning for Dane County around 6:00 p.m. These types of tornado watches and warnings happened so often now that Steve just nodded in acknowledgment. Not only were they common, but he teased Sally about being a worrywart, too.

Before Steve pulled out of the garage, he jokingly told Sally, "Hey, have a big party while we're gone!"—it was one of the few times he'd ventured out with the kids, and she'd have the house to herself. She daydreamed of having a good, long run on the treadmill. Though she had been away from her children for short stints before, they were used to being together as a family! In fact, the Lovells ran a business selling plastics processing equipment, robots, and injection molding machines out of an office in their home, so for Sally to be in the house alone without anyone was a rare event.

Glass Storm

The kids whined once again, pleading to stay back with Sally and Madi, the family dog.

She instead blew them kisses and waved, saying, "I love you. See you soon. Dad's appointment to give blood only takes about an hour. Don't worry! You'll be back before you know it."

The kids were lulled into the car with the promise of cookies and juice, and off they went. As Sally watched the kids drive away, she turned back to the matter at hand: making a casserole to take to the funeral reception. Her mind wandered to a time when a casserole had been delivered to them, the day they returned home from the hospital with Stephen. This night stuck out because as soon as the neighbors left, there was a tornado warning.

They'd already taught Mary how to be prepared for the worst type of storms. She immediately ran to grab her tornado survival kit from the closet below the living room stairs. Inside the Tupperware kit was bottled water, a blanket, granola bars, a flashlight, batteries, a first-aid kit, a coloring book with crayons, dog food, and extra shoes.

"Mary, where should we go for this storm?" Sally asked.

"To the basement, away from glass windows, Mom."

Steve quickly packed up the meal, and everyone headed downstairs to the basement. That night, the family slept in the unfinished room together, Madi close by, while the storm continued to rage. Baby Stephen nestled into his car seat to sleep, still in that newborn sleepy bliss, unaware of what might be happening. That storm blew past without causing damage to the Lovells' home. But they knew there would be more thunderstorms and tornado warnings.

Sally snapped back into the present. She needed to iron Stephen's suit and get everyone packed up for their drive back to Menominee, Michigan, to her hometown, for the funeral of a close family friend. She couldn't help but wonder: when was the last time she had seen Mary's tornado survival kit?

~~~

As the car pulled out, Mary's eyes paused at the For Sale sign in the yard. "Hey, Dad?" she asked. "Do you think we'll move anytime soon?"

"I guess I'm not sure. Why, are you in a hurry to get away from this place?"

Steve laughed.

~ ~ ~

Back inside the kitchen, Sally watched the local news. A list of colorful warnings and watches scrolled across the bottom of the screen for Dane County. A Madison meteorologist began zooming in on individual rotations. Sally became concerned when he said, "Fitchburg" and "headed in the path of Stoughton." Fitchburg was only about fifteen miles away, a direct path toward Stoughton. Sally began to panic. The meteorologist kept using timelines. Most tornadoes occur between 4:00 p.m. and 9:00 p.m. A funnel cloud—a rotating cloud that allows a tornado to touch ground—had been spotted in Fitchburg around 6:20 p.m.

It was prime tornado season in Tornado Alley.

Chapter 2

Built From the Ground Up

August 18, 2005 had been a scorching hot day in Wisconsin, one of those days that you could practically see the concrete sizzling in the sun. Mary, age 9, and Stephen, age 7, ran gleefully through the spray of the water sprinkler, doing their best to enjoy the dwindling days of summer vacation. Their parents, Sally and Steve, looked on contentedly, unaware of the course of destruction that was set to turn their city, their house, and their lives upside down.

~ ~ ~

Sally and her husband Steve, along with their children Mary and Stephen, lived in Stoughton, Wisconsin, Town of Pleasant Springs, a city proud of its Norwegian heritage. There's a Syttende Mai parade in honor of Norwegian Constitution Day, held every year on the weekend closest to May 17. Sally and Steve appreciated the educational aspects of living in a town that prided itself on its heritage and ensured the kids were involved in as many activities as possible. That included a parade, traditional music, a canoe race down the Yahara River, athletic events, and cookouts, just to name a few.

Mary's favorite activity was rosemaling, traditional Norwegian folk painting of swirly flowers. Girls in Mary's class wore bunads, traditional embroidered Norwegian costumes with long, flowing, black skirts, red bonnets, and white blouses with red vests during the week at school in preparation for Syttende Mai. Some even had matching outfits for their dolls.

Stephen enjoyed running the two-mile Lil' Syttende Mai community race and walk with his friends and earning a colorful T-shirt for participating. He also liked hanging out at the finish line to cheer on those who ran twenty miles from the state capitol in Madison. The top finishers of the twenty-mile race receive hand-painted Norwegian rosemaled gifts. Stephen and Mary loved cheering on their mother as she crossed the finish line after the long run.

The Stoughton Public Library offered summer reading programs that rewarded kids with prizes such as butterfly nets, extra books, and cool water bottles. There were even tokens for free food and ice cream at local eateries. The program had special activities each week, and Mary and Stephen especially loved going around the corner to Fosdal Home Bakery after story time to pick out a frosted cut-out sugar cookie.

The Lovell kids also enjoyed meeting up with friends at Eugster's Farm Market and Petting Farm. Eugster's usually was open early spring until shortly after Halloween. There, the kids were able to hold kittens, feed baby goats ice cream cones full of food pellets, and race each other on the tractor trikes and miniature farm equipment. The kids enjoyed picking pumpkins in the fall to carve jack-o'-lanterns for Halloween and taking hayrides on the back of a tractor. Sally and her friends packed lunches to eat at Eugster's picnic tables with all their kids. Eugster's even offered a farmers' market with local fresh fruits and vegetables for sale. No trip was complete unless they came home with a fresh apple pie.

~ ~ ~

Steve and Sally built their home from the ground up in 1997. They'd chosen the lot because it was close to town and had a large yard for Mary, Stephen, and Madi, their family dog. It sat high on a hill overlooking Lake Kegonsa, and the Lovells could see the state capitol from their kitchen window. On the Fourth of July, neighbors and friends gathered outside with their lawn chairs while blasting their radios to patriotic music during the fireworks display. It was always a fun neighborhood celebration.

At night during the summer, the kids could hear the frogs croaking and the crickets chirping loudly. Mary and Stephen caught fireflies in the twilight with their butterfly nets. One night, they put the fireflies in a glass jar with air holes, and Stephen fell asleep with them next to his bed, a magical night-light. He released the fireflies in the morning. Mud wasps would make their nests nearby on the hot brick house after collecting mud from Lake Kegonsa. Mary went to get the mail one afternoon after returning home from dance class, wearing a ballerina leotard. She opened the small mailbox door and a huge cloud of wasps flew out at her! A couple got stuck in her leotard, stinging her armpit multiple times.

The backyard of their house butted up against the cornfield, and across from their lot was a large, weathered, red barn. The Lovells' lot had been a gigantic cornfield until the owners sold it to a developer. The corn was generally knee high by the Fourth of July, and soon it would be harvested and used as feed for livestock.

Mary and Stephen enjoyed the big, noisy, dusty, robust farming machinery that buzzed right up next to their house. The owners of the land always gave a big wave as they passed by. After all the stalks were gone, the land became lifeless again until the following spring when the planting cycle began anew.

CHAPTER 3

The Phone Call

All the way on the other side of town, Steve was preparing to donate blood. As a regular blood donor, he knew the routine. In the waiting room, his mind wandered to the question that Mary had asked in the car. Would they move soon? They'd talked about moving to the city, but he did love the farmland that surrounded them.

Just then, a volunteer interrupted his thoughts, calling his name to head back to the donor room. Steve handed Mary his cell phone. "You can answer this if anyone calls. If it's something important, come get me."

Another volunteer came to show Mary and Stephen to a room with tables full of snacks, candy, and drinks. A kid's dream! They dug in and waited patiently, unaware of what was going on all the way on the other side of town.

~ ~ ~

Back in Stoughton, Madi, who generally seemed content lying in her dog bed, had begun running in and out of Sally's legs. She was panting uncontrollably, shaking and agitated. Madi was usually happy to just be in her bed. Something was wrong.

Sally gently scratched Madi's back. "Go lie down, Madi. You're acting crazy."

Again, the dog brushed up against Sally, this time poking her wet muzzle in front of Sally's legs.

"Go lie down!" Sally insisted.

But it seemed to her like Madi was trying to tell her something. Madi always listened to Sally's commands. At that moment, Sally looked out the north-facing kitchen window and glanced down the hill at Lake Kegonsa. It was eerie outside, and the darkness reflected off the lake. Confused, she looked again. It had been sunny, warm, and clear all day. Why were there suddenly huge, black clouds?

She ran and opened the front door, which faced the Stoughton Country Club, to see what was happening, thinking it was just a thunderstorm rolling in.

Then she saw it, and drew her breath. There was a tornado barreling down the fairway, right toward her house.

Sally strained to see the fairway and watched a golfer in a golf cart speeding toward her neighbor's house to take shelter. She slammed the front door, as if that act alone could keep the tornado away. Sally felt like she was going to die. It was the scariest, most violent, and most powerful storm she'd ever witnessed. The cloud was fierce and monstrous, with black-and-white pieces of debris that looked just like black-and-white birds circling their prey. The funnel looked at least a mile high, with a notch in the top. It was as though a double tornado was headed right toward her, coming to swallow her and Madi. Sally couldn't tell what the dark and light structures whirling around were in the sky, but she knew they were coming toward her, and she didn't want to stick around any longer to find out. Her heart was pounding, and her stomach was knotted.

Sally and Mary Lovell

This is it! Sally thought as her adrenaline kicked in.

She suddenly knew, with conviction, that she did not want to die this way. She swiftly picked up the dog, who was trying to climb her like a ladder. She grabbed her phone and sprinted to the basement. As soon as she closed the door, she grabbed her phone and fumbled to use the walkie-talkie connection to intercom with Mary. Sally was crying but remained calm as she knew she had to say goodbye.

~~~

Over in Madison, the walkie-talkie function of her father's phone started to go off, chirping like crazy, so Mary grabbed it. It was her mom, but Mary couldn't hear her very well, so she pulled up the small black antenna on the phone and walked toward the window in hopes of better reception. By the time she clicked the walkie-talkie back, she could hear her mom again.

"Honey, I love you, and I think I'm going to die. There's a tornado coming toward the house."

~ ~ ~

She just barely finished her sentence when the connection ended. Sally looked down at her trembling hands, wondering if that would be the last time she would ever speak to her daughter again. Should she try to call again, or would it be better to say nothing at all?

CHAPTER 4

The Storm

As fast as she could, Sally grabbed Madi and raced down to the basement. She backed herself into the corner of the basement, under the wrought-iron table near the metal Bilco door, the wide, heavy door that led from the ground to the basement. She checked to be sure she was away from any shelves. The life-size snowman decoration was sitting on top of the table because it was too tall for the shelves. She wondered if the extra weight would help hold the table in place. Sally was on her hands and knees with Madi, shaking in fear. She was out of breath from the terror and tried to slow her breathing by counting to five so she wouldn't hyperventilate.

It didn't take long until she could hear the strong

wind banging against the Bilco basement doors. She looked at the glass block windows in the wells closest to her, and it was still dark from the storm. Her mind flashed to all the tiger salamanders and toads and frogs that Stephen had saved from those same window wells. Where was he now? Would she have the chance to watch him rescue them ever again?

Sally knew she wasn't safe here, and she could feel herself being pulled toward the windows by the powerful winds circulating above her. She closed her eyes and prayed, "Dear God, please let me survive this storm so I can see my family again. Please keep Steve and Mary and Stephen safe, wherever they are. I'll do anything to see them again. Please."

~~~

Meanwhile, in Madison, Mary clutched the phone and raced down the hallway toward her dad. She flung open the door and screamed, "Mom said there's a tornado heading straight for the house and she thinks she's going to die. Please save her, Dad! Please save her!"

The nurse had been ready to stick the needle in Steve's right arm, but he bolted from the chair, ripping off all the tape and cords. He grabbed his children, one in each arm like Superman, and ran to the elevators. The ride down seemed to last forever, but they finally reached the car. Steve kept trying to reach Sally while he drove, but she never answered.

~ ~ ~

Sally wiggled out from under the metal table with Madi in her arms and sprinted across the basement to the bathroom shower. It sounded like the Bilco doors were being ripped off their hinges. She frantically hunkered down on the cold shower floor over Madi. Sally covered her head with her hands to protect herself from flying debris, but her ears began popping from the changing air pressure, so she moved her palms over her ears. She knew the tornado was overhead, and she screamed in terror.

Sally heard a constant thud of objects hitting the house and crashes from upstairs. The garage doors were pounding, and she could hear them fold under the pressure from the immense winds, almost as though the metal doors were giant pop cans being crushed. Windows were exploding. The ground beneath her trembled. The sound of a freight train whirled around above her.

Even with a tornado attacking the house, Sally was so grateful for the presence of her faithful dog, Madi. They shared an exceptional bond. When Sally was a few months pregnant, she decided it was a good time to get a dog. A pet would keep her company while Steve was traveling for work and would be a companion for their future child.

Sally grew up with dogs, usually two at a time. Labs and schnauzers were her family's dogs of choice. She'd dress the dogs in Halloween costumes, throw tea parties for them, and let them sleep in her bed at night. Sally wanted her kids to experience the companionship, love, and warmth dogs bring to a family. After all, dogs are miracle workers—they seem to be placed in their owners' lives for a specific purpose.

Sally had located a litter of Miniature Schnauzers up for adoption. However, on the day she went to adopt Madi, Steve was out of town for work. He reluctantly told her to pick one, knowing that his wife seemed intent on doing this. The adoption center only took cash, so Sally went to the bank to take out a $500 loan without telling her husband. She knew he wouldn't mind, but usually they did things like that together, and Sally hadn't noticed the enormous finance charge on the loan. When Steve found out, he paid it off within hours, his love for Sally overcoming his reluctance to have a pet.

Sally and her best friend drove together to Milwaukee to get her new dog. Worried about whether a male dog would mark its territory, she chose a good-tempered, salt-and-pepper-colored female and called her Madison, or Madi for short.

Madi had been the protector of Mary and Stephen their whole lives, watching their every move for nearly ten years. The day Sally brought her home, she was about the size of a guinea pig. The green grass was so tall that it tickled Madi's belly. The grass looked like a jungle compared to her short legs. Mary was born three months later, and the pair became instant companions. Wherever Sally took Mary, Madi was always close behind, usually carrying a chew toy and wagging her tail. She loved having the new addition of Stephen a few years later.

The Lovells treated Madi like a family member, like a third child. As soon as the kids opened their bedroom doors in the morning, Madi heard their feet pitter-patter on the floor and ran to alert Sally they were coming. Stephen would run down the stairs and hide under the dining room table, hoping his mom wouldn't see him. Madi would bark the second she heard him. Madi sat next to them on the floor while the kids played together.

~~~

Steve and the kids sped down their usual route home to Stoughton. Steve tuned in the local radio station, 1310 AM, for updates on the storm. He was worried how his kids would react to seeing their house and wanted to be armed with as much information as possible beforehand.

For the fifteen-mile drive home, Mary held to the hope that her mother had made it out of the house. With her eyes closed, scenes ran through her mind like a movie montage. She pictured a tornado ripping through her house like the weather stations on TV always showed. Stephen cried, unable to comprehend what was happening.

It was the first time ever that Mary heard her dad swear as he tried repeatedly to get his wife to answer the phone. Still in shock, Mary just sat quietly behind the driver's seat, trying not to cry and avoiding the thoughts of life without her mom.

As they turned a corner, Steve said to himself, "Well, we might be moving sooner rather than later."

Mary felt her stomach sink.

~ ~ ~

To Sally, the tornado seemed to last a lifetime. Car alarms and sirens blared in the distance, but finally she stopped hearing the horrifying sounds of the storm. She felt humidity like never before, and the heat wafted down the basement stairway. She was still on top of Madi, her hands over her head. The air around her was warm and stuffy, and the basement was dark. She knew the power was definitely out because the air conditioning was no longer running and she'd turned on the lights when she ran downstairs.

Uninjured but in shock, she slowly started to move her hands off her head and felt Madi's tiny heart pounding as she drew her closer for comfort. The sweet pup's legs were shaking uncontrollably, as though she'd suffered through a night of Fourth of July fireworks. Without letting go of her trembling companion, Sally got to her knees to look around.

As Sally slowly began to make her way up the stairs, she attempted to prepare herself for the aftermath. She knew to expect broken windows or worse when she went upstairs. What she saw was beyond her worst nightmare.

CHAPTER 5

There's No Way In

"Sally! Sally! Are you there?" Steve yelled desperately.

Sally held the phone close to her mouth, but no words came out. Everything was fuzzy. She wasn't thinking clearly enough to put a real sentence together, although she tried.

~ ~ ~

"Sally? Sally, are you there?" Steve tried again.

Mary looked up, catching a quick glimpse into her father's eyes. From the looks of the neighborhood so far, she was more certain than ever that her mom had died. Parts of their hometown looked like a bomb had been set off—and someone had thrown gas on it to make it explode a second time. She wasn't even sure if they'd ever be able to *find* their mom. Her heart sank as she imagined life with just the three of them, without her mom. She'd have to step up more around the house, she decided. She'd do the cooking, maybe the laundry.

~ ~ ~

Sally finally pressed the walkie-talkie button on the phone. "I can't move," she said.

"Did something fall on you?" Steve asked. "Where are you? We'll be there as soon as we can. We just need to know where you are."

Sally's body was shaking with more fear than she had ever experienced. She still struggled to find words. She didn't know how to explain to her family the magnitude of what had just happened. She managed to say enough to reassure Steve that she was alive, that she would be okay.

~ ~ ~

In the back seat, Mary felt relieved. But more than that, she wanted to tear the phone from her father and talk with her mom. Just then, Stephen, now even more confused and frightened about his mother's whereabouts, started to cry harder. Mary reached over, but nothing was going to comfort him except seeing her.

How could something like this happen? they wondered.

After what seemed like an eternity, Steve and the children reached their subdivision, only to find every entrance blocked with debris. Trees had been uprooted and thrown like javelins, houses they'd passed by every day for years were leveled, power lines were down, and cars were overturned from the force of the storm. People and pets were climbing out of ditches on the side of the road where they'd hidden from the tornado.

Mary knew the storm had left, but the weather remained muggy and hazy. All the sirens scared her—she knew sirens meant something bad was taking place. Her stomach felt queasy, and her heart was pounding. Mary fought tears as she looked over at Stephen, whose eyes were bloodshot from crying. Mary took his hand this time.

"Is Mommy going to die?" he whimpered.

The route they'd driven out on an hour earlier was blocked by fallen debris. Police cars, fire trucks, and ambulances with flashing lights took up the rest of the road. As Steve and the kids reached Highway B, just a few minutes away, they found the road blocked with flashing lights and a police officer guarding the road. Steve's stomach knotted, and Mary and Stephen began to cry even harder. The reality of what had happened was finally setting in.

Steve had been hopeful the storm wasn't as bad as Sally had described. He'd been praying it was just a bad windstorm. But when he pulled up next to an officer holding an orange flare in his hand, he knew better. Steve rolled down the window as he approached.

"Sir, you need to turn around," the officer called out. "The road is closed."

"I can't turn around. I'm on my way home. I need to get home. We live on Sheryl Lane. My wife was in the tornado. All alone. We need to get there NOW."

"I'm sorry, but you'll need to find another route. I suggest Highway 51. It will take you about an hour—

traffic is really backed up on the back side of Lake Kegonsa."

Frustrated, Steve pulled a U-turn and headed back on Highway N. There they picked up Interstate 90 for a few miles and then got on Highway 12/18, also known as the Beltline. It seemed like forever before they exited onto Stoughton Road/Highway 51. Shortly after McFarland, the traffic came to a crawl. It was solid red taillights all the way to Stoughton.

Steve kept reassuring the kids that Sally was okay. "What's the first thing you'll do when you see Mom?" he asked.

"I'm going to run as fast as I can to hug her," Mary said.

"I'm going to run faster than Mary and jump up into her arms!" Stephen said.

"We can't forget about Madi," Steve said. "What will you do when you see her?"

"I'll hug her tight!" Stephen shouted excitedly.

Steve felt a warm flood of emotion. His heart was full of love for his family. However, he knew they still needed to find Sally and make sure she was safe. He couldn't imagine raising the kids and going through life without his best friend. He needed to see for himself that she was okay.

CHAPTER 6

Glass Everywhere

Flipping into survival mode, Sally grabbed her running shoes from the spot next to the treadmill where she always left them after her workout. Today, she was especially grateful for them because she hadn't been wearing shoes when she ran for cover in the basement. She quickly put them on and made her way upstairs, glad she wouldn't encounter any broken objects barefoot.

Sally felt a lump in her throat, and tears streamed down her face as she approached the last step. She was scared of seeing the aftermath. The electricity had not come back on. Sally reached the hallway atop the basement stairs. It was windowless, and the silence in the room felt eerie. She braced herself for what was to come.

Crunch! Glass was everywhere. The first thing she thought was that she would look up into the first floor of the house and see the sky with the roof and everything else gone. However, it was even worse than she imagined—she could see her beloved items still in the house, only the majority of them had been destroyed.

Sally forced herself to take a few more steps to enter the kitchen and find the nearest door. She was filled with emotion because it looked as though an explosion had taken place in her house. The kitchen window that framed a picture-perfect view of Lake Kegonsa had been blown out, along with its wooden trim and blinds. A metal lawn chair from outside had blown through the window and was sitting in the corner near a built-in china hutch.

The Corian countertop, which was nonporous and heat- and scratch-resistant, had severe gashes across it as though bears had attacked it. The cord for the red toaster was still plugged into the wall, but the toaster lay smashed on its side. The hand-glazed red teapot Mary and Stephen had given her for Mother's Day lay shattered next to it.

As her eyes continued to skim, Sally saw the scotcheroo pan, lodged upside down underneath the refrigerator. Sally recalled Stephen asking for a scotcheroo earlier that day. Why did she wait to give Stephen one? What if that had been the last chance she'd ever have to make a scotcheroo for her son? What if…? She was frustrated, thinking about how life was too short. All she wanted was to be reunited with her family. Tears streamed down her face.

Sally took another step into the kitchen, noticing the construction paper thumbprint angel Stephen had made her for Mother's Day just a few months prior. A circular clay disk the size of a cookie made up the head. Stephen's thumbprint made impressions for the eyes and mouth, which were painted blue and red. The body was cut from blue construction paper, and the words *Made with love by: Stephen* were written on the front. Brown yarn was used for hair, and a long piece of string attached the head to the light fixture. Even though the fixture had been pulled from the ceiling and only hung by a few wires, the thumbprint angel was still hanging by its yarn, perfectly intact. How had something so fragile survived the storm?

Sally thought how unfathomable it was that just moments earlier, fierce winds had been roaring through the house and hallways where she stood. Sally began to cry again, this time even harder. Madi was still shaking and panting, her pink tongue hanging out. Sally opened the front door frantically and ran down the driveway steps, fearing the fate of her neighbors. Then she caught the first glimpse of her once-beautiful neighborhood. She froze and didn't know what to do next. She wanted to close her eyes and discover this was just a bad dream, but reality set in when her phone rang.

"What's happening?" Steve asked her. "I'm worried about you. Are you okay? I have the kids, and we're on our way to the house."

"I'm out of the house," Sally managed. "I'm safe."

~ ~ ~

Steve knew he wouldn't be able to drive all the way home, but he was going to do his best to get them as close as possible. He exited on Schneider Drive and cut alongside the lake. He managed to reach the back of the

Stoughton Country Club on Brooklyn Drive. He pulled to a stop on the golf course. They had no choice but to abandon the car and run across the fairway of the country club, where Mary and Stephen had taken junior golf lessons.

~~~

Outside on Sheryl Lane, Sally met up with a neighbor who was just as frazzled as she was. They squeezed each other into a tight, long hug as tears streamed down their cheeks. Sally and her neighbor were familiar with neighbors' cars and work schedules, and so they decided to go door-to-door to take inventory of the neighbors that should be home. They started by counting cars.

It was a difficult task as some of the garages had crushed the cars inside and others had been scattered about. From across the way, they heard another neighbor hollering, "Are you okay? Where are you?" to Sally's next-door neighbors. She looked next door and spotted a car in the driveway. Sally knew her next-door neighbor's daughter and grandkids were staying at the house while her parents were on vacation. Sally and her neighbor walked across the torn-up lawn to the driveway to meet the other neighbor. After yelling a few more times, they heard voices from the basement.

The home's large trusses had collapsed, and the basement was blocked. Instantly, they knew they had to help. With their bare hands, they dug through the twisted debris until the neighbors were free.

The daughter came up carrying the kids, all of them with fear on their faces. She said that when the windows had begun exploding, she'd run with the kids to the basement. She'd thrown herself atop them while the storm raged. Just like Sally, she had a hard time moving afterward because of how traumatic the experience had been.

Unbelievably, no one was injured and everyone was accounted for on Sheryl Lane.

Amid the remains of a totaled house, someone noticed a Bible sitting perfectly on a fireplace mantel. The rest of the room was ruined, but the Bible didn't have a blemish on it. In a few days, the governor of Wisconsin would come to the neighborhood and have a look at the Bible for himself.

One neighbor solved the problem of blocked roads by barreling through the cornfield in an SUV. He and his family had only lived in their house for a few months, and it was a complete loss.

Thank goodness they weren't home, Sally thought.

Other neighbors called out for their lost pets, cries that made Sally especially sad. She was still holding Madi in her arms even though they ached from the weight of the fifteen-pound dog. She counted her blessings that Madi had alerted her of the coming storm and saved Sally from being critically injured—or worse. Madi was her own personal superhero. The storm had hit just as many neighbors arrived home from work—their first item of business had been to let the family pet out. The storm came so quickly there hadn't been time to get their pets back inside to safety.

She watched as one of her neighbors ran to each house to shut off the gas and prevent any possibility of an explosion. Incredibly, their instincts kicked in and they all got to work. After all, it wasn't like the neighborhood had gotten special catastrophe training.

~ ~ ~

As Steve and the kids approached the country club's dining room, they were met with their first up-close view of the destruction. The dining room roof looked like it had been picked straight up and dropped, causing it to cave in. There was debris everywhere.

Mary stared horrified at the huge snapped-in-half trees and the demolished fairway. "Dad, do you think we'll ever be able to play golf here again?"

Steve didn't answer. He didn't know what to say. He just kept his family moving, increasingly desperate to find his wife.

They ran down the tattered fairway and made it to Shadyside Lane, finding it walkable.

Mary was wearing sparkly blue flip-flops, and suddenly she realized she was stepping on shattered glass and razor-sharp splintered wood. "Ouch!" she cried.

Steve looked at her bloody feet but knew there was little he could do empty-handed. "We're almost home, and we need to find Mom. Can you be strong for me so we can make sure she's safe?"

"You got it, Dad." Mary knew her mom was in danger, and all thoughts of Band-Aids quickly left her mind. She needed her mother more.

The family passed shredded trees, shards of wood jammed everywhere. The air was so heavy and humid that it was difficult to breathe, especially while running. Mary noticed there weren't any birds singing. For a while, she questioned if they were even running in the right direction—absolutely nothing looked familiar. All around were sounds of people screaming and crying because their entire lives had changed. Steve had to give Stephen a piggyback ride because his little legs were too tired for the long trek.

Finally, the neighborhood began to look recognizable. Mary looked to her right and saw the sign for the street she'd grown up on. "We're almost home, Dad!" she shouted as the Sheryl Lane street sign and the shiny black granite marquee for Greenbriar Estates came into view at the bottom of the hill. Mary sighed in relief at how close they were. At the same time, she wasn't mentally prepared to see her mom, the house, or their street.

None of them were.

Steve took Mary's hand firmly and set Stephen down. They stood for a moment, staring up at the hill where they had such warm memories. In the summer, they rolled down the hill like sacks of potatoes and watched as the older neighborhood boys did downhill tricks on their bikes. Birthday parties were celebrated outside, eating on the patio with Madi running around them. Christmas lights filled the snowy trees during the holidays while the kids sledded down the hill. Everyone had a reason to climb up the hill on Sheryl Lane to see what the raging storm had done to their home.

And then they saw Sally running toward them, still holding Madi so she wouldn't cut her feet. They locked eyes and ran toward one another.

CHAPTER 7

What's Left?

When the Lovell family finally reunited, they weren't sure who ran fastest to hug one another. Everyone held on as tightly as they could with tears flowing down their faces. Mary hugged her mom's waist, and Stephen held her leg. Steve put his arms around everyone, including Madi. No one wanted to let go of Sally. The kids' cheeks were flushed from the long walk. Sweat trickled down the side of Steve's face. Mary's feet were covered in blood.

They finally took a step back and turned to stare at the chaotic scene around them in utter disbelief.

"Thank God we're all okay; that's all that matters," Steve told his family.

Stephen held tightly to his mother's hand while Sally

passed Madi to Mary. No one wanted her paws to get cut on the glass, so for the time being, they took turns holding her.

The Lovells walked up the hill to get to their home and take inventory of what was missing and what remained intact. The air was heavy. They could hear their neighbors' heartbreaking voices still calling for lost pets. They held Madi close, so grateful to not have to live life without her. Several of the neighbors' houses were nothing but heaps of bricks and rubble, two-by-fours, insulation, and broken glass.

"What happened to the neighbor's dog?" Stephen asked. "Why are they yelling for him?"

"He just got scared and ran away," Sally said. "He'll be home soon." She didn't know how to explain that many pets surely had been killed by the storm.

The first thing Mary noticed was their dismantled wrought-iron mailbox. Its 1860 address marker and little golfer medallion were on the ground. The For Sale sign was reduced to just a jagged post. The family stared at the once-perfect home. Every window in the two-story, red-brick house was cracked, scratched, or missing entirely.

And somehow, embedded in the side of the roof above the garage, was a giant, shiny steering wheel. The Lovells later learned that the steering wheel had come from a boat in Lake Kegonsa. The magnitude of the storm and the complexity of its winds to put the steering wheel there only reinforced their belief of how lucky Sally was to take cover in the basement when she did.

Trees were toppled, and lawn furniture they didn't even recognize was smashed against the corner of the house. Sally's beautiful white hydrangeas were ripped from the ground. Dried cornstalks littered the yard. Although the house was standing, no one knew if it was structurally safe, or what other damage awaited them inside.

As soon as he could, Steve called the family's insurance agent. He lived less than a mile away and showed up quickly with a first-aid kit. Not wasting a minute, he first assessed the family for injuries, getting to work on tending to Mary's feet. He explained to the family that they had a policy, but they weren't sure what was covered due to the extent of the damage. He advised them not to enter the house until a building inspector could assess the damage. The Lovells had purchased insurance years earlier, knowing that bad things can happen, but they'd never have dreamed it could be as bad as this.

The family stood there with a realization that they were essentially homeless.

CHAPTER 8

Evacuation

The mighty oak that once stood tall at the end of Sheryl Lane and Linnerud Drive had been stripped of foliage. Mary and Stephen had spent many hours there, playing on the large boulders that surrounded the tree and searching for bugs with butterfly nets. There was no more shelter from the sunshine—just the trunk and a few branches remained. The oak almost appeared naked without its graceful outstretched limbs and beautiful vegetation. Some of the heavy boulders that lay beneath it were missing as well.

Sally felt devastation well up in her again as she looked at the tree that had been so much a part of their lives. During summer, she would pack lunches of peanut butter sandwiches, chocolate chip cookies, and fruit to eat under the tree. Her career as a teacher had allowed for summers at home, and then later being the office manager of their family business had allowed her flexible hours. She was eternally grateful to have had plenty of time to devote to her children and to their business. She'd put Stephen and Madi in the wagon, and Mary would help pull them down the street. They'd sit under the tree on a blanket, eating, reading, and simply enjoying the moment. They discussed the importance of eating their fruits and vegetables so they could grow up and one day be as big and strong as the tree.

One day, a bunch of red ants bit Mary. From then on, she took her own camping chair to sit on, though the ants still found her anyway. Acorns littered the grass below the tree. The scampering of squirrels running up and down the tree shook loose more acorns, which occasionally hit Mary or Stephen on the head.

When grandparents came to visit, they'd walk to the oak with the kids. When Sally was training for a triathlon, Mary biked to the tree and back as fast as she could and had her mother time her. Once, a red fox was living in the giant rocks under the tree. Stephen was petrified because he thought the animal was the real-life Swiper the Fox from *Dora the Explorer*.

~ ~ ~

Nightfall came. The Lovells still didn't know exactly what had hit them because the neighborhood remained without electricity. A group of neighbors gathered at Sheryl Lane and Linnerud Drive to try to decide what to do. The smell of natural gas laced the air.

Residents couldn't leave because of damaged cars and roads, but more importantly, they didn't want to leave for fear of people stealing their belongings. *Then again*, they thought, *who would want any of it? And what would they do to scare them off anyway?* It was more the principle that everything they owned was buried somewhere in that house, if not gone. They didn't want to leave it because they didn't know when they could come back, or if they could. The neighborhood was a complete and utter disaster area.

Sally and Steve were sitting on their front steps trying to decide what to do. Should they stay outside all night and stand guard? Or should they walk in the pitch black to Steve's car a half hour away? They knew it wasn't safe to enter the home, but they knew they wouldn't sleep anyway because of the turmoil and uncertainty. Steve and Sally knew there was no way out and no way in. Any decision meant leaving something behind.

Steve spotted a sheriff's deputy slowly driving up the hill on Sheryl Lane, blue and red lights flashing atop the squad car.

The deputy, dressed in his dark brown and tan uniform, pulled the car to the side of the road. Then he stepped out and held up a black megaphone. "Please gather any belongings. You must evacuate the premises."

Steve and Sally looked at one another in disbelief. Before they could say anything, the megaphone sputtered again.

"The National Guard has been dispatched. You will be allowed back in sometime tomorrow. Part of your neighborhood has been declared a state of emergency."

An immediate evacuation had been ordered. Stephen and Mary clasped Sally's hand in fear. Tears began to well up in Sally's eyes.

"What does 'evacuate' mean?" Stephen asked.

"We have to leave our house now," Sally said. "It's not safe."

The decision had been made for the Lovells.

As neighbors stood in the street, the deputy told them to grab anything of importance that they could carry. They'd be allowed to return the next day if it was safe. What was the family supposed to do when Steve's car was miles away and Sally's car was inside the toppled garage? Where were they going to go?

The deputy offered to take them to Steve's car. They left quickly with only the clothes on their backs. They didn't grab a thing. Even Madi got to ride in the police car. Steve sat in the front, and the kids climbed in the back with Sally, Madi on her lap.

Sally felt herself shaking, and tears ran down her cheeks. Mary reached for her hand. Sally had tried to be convincing for her children, but she truly had no idea what tomorrow—or even tonight—would bring.

They took one last look at their battered home as the deputy began to drive into the pitch-black night. Steve and the deputy made small talk, but otherwise, the car ride was quiet.

All they could see was devastation. It didn't matter the size or structure of the house. Large and small, they'd been hammered. If something had been in the way of the tornado, it was obliterated. Black asphalt was ripped from roads, giant trees were busted right down the middle, and wooden telephone poles lined the streets. Debris was everywhere. The whole subdivision was black, no power anywhere.

The deputy was kind, calming, and comforting, something that the family desperately needed. He assured them that the National Guard had already been deployed, and soldiers would be arriving soon to help. His presence alone made this moment survivable, his compassion and strength something that would stick with each and every Lovell for years to come.

The family reached Steve's car, where they thanked the deputy for his help. Without him, they would have been trapped in a danger zone.

CHAPTER 9

Homeless

The Lovells had no home to go home to. Mary and Stephen wouldn't be able to fall asleep without their baby blankets. Madi didn't have her dog bed to curl up in. Sally didn't have her wedding ring. They didn't have cell phone chargers. Not even a toothbrush. All their documents for the house and business—everything—were somewhere inside their broken house or lost. They were homeless.

Still, they needed someplace to stay. Steve began driving toward Madison on Highway 51. The surrounding neighborhoods had been ordered to evacuate, too, and every hotel seemed to be full. After checking a few places, it seemed like the family might be sleeping in the car.

The kids hadn't eaten since the cookies and brownies at the Red Cross, so Steve pulled through an Arby's drive-thru. Although Steve and Sally felt too sick to their stomachs to eat, the kids ordered their favorites, curly fries and chicken tenders, to stop their tummies from rumbling. There was a Days Inn hotel nearby, and not only did they have a room, they even took Madi. In the Lovells went, no suitcases, no luggage, and no toys—just the clothes they wore. Sally realized Madi hadn't been able to walk around for several hours, so she took the dog outside on the dark-green, glass-free grass.

The room had a king bed and a pullout couch for the kids. Mary's feet were still bleeding, so Sally had her take a shower to get cleaned up. Sally also got toothbrushes and more bandages from the front desk and a plastic bowl from the hotel kitchen so she could give Madi some water. Steve put sheets and pillows on the pullout bed and set a large towel in the center for the kids to eat on. They plopped down and ate while watching TV.

For a moment, life seemed back to normal. They were all still running on adrenaline. It was well past midnight before Steve and Sally made the kids shut off the TV.

Just before they turned to fall asleep, Mary said, "Mom? Dad? I don't even care if we don't have a house. All that matters is that we are all here, all together."

While the kids slept, Steve and Sally sat in bed, working through their disbelief to discuss who they should call and what they should do. All night, they called relatives and friends. Sally's parents didn't believe her at first until she told them to turn on the TV. Many relatives and friends already had seen the news reports, so word spread quickly. A few of them even watched it unfold, live.

As Mary and Stephen struggled to fall asleep in their strange surroundings, they could hear the soft murmurs of their dad on the phone. "Who do you think he's talking to?" Stephen asked. Mary listened a moment, and then answered, "I bet it's Grandpa Gary. Dad always feels better when he talks to Grandpa."

Steve and Sally stayed awake, talking the entire night, with Madi close by. Already, Sally made it clear that they would NOT be moving back into the house—that was for sure. Besides, would there even be a house to move back into? Plus, the trauma she'd experienced had left her emotionally scarred. Was this a sign it was time to move for good to Michigan?

How would the kids do? They had to decide things quickly because school would be starting in just a few weeks. The kids were happy with their friends and schools. What about their business? Steve didn't know how they could keep it going—everything needed to run the operation had been inside their home office, now in shambles. So many questions remained unanswered.

At 5:00 a.m., Steve and Sally turned on the TV to watch the local news. The images on the TV looked even worse than what they remembered—daylight exposed the truth. Many helicopters shared aerial coverage. As one camera zoomed in on the Lovells' neighborhood, Sally again felt a deep gratitude that she hadn't been injured.

The couple quickly woke the kids. They were anxious to get back to the house and assess the damage. But first, they made their way to the hotel breakfast. Stephen was excited because he loved hotel waffle makers. The minute they left their room, the smell of waffles filled the hall.

Stephen smiled. "I wonder if they have chocolate chips!"

Many of their Stoughton neighbors also had spent the night at Days Inn and greeted the Lovells with their own stories. Sadly, they learned that one of their neighbors had died when his chimney fell on him while he was seeking shelter in the basement, and twenty-three others were injured. One family had ended up driving toward the tornado instead of away from it because of its unpredictability. One man had just placed more disaster insurance on his business the day before the tornado hit. A couple eating dinner saw a lawn mower fly past their lawn, only to see a tornado directly behind it.

They heard a story of a family that lost their house completely. A father and son had just gotten home from football practice and ran to the basement. The father ran back upstairs to get the dog, but saw the tornado coming toward the house. He had a decision to make: grab the dog or run back inside to save his own life. After a split second, he ran downstairs and took shelter next to his son behind the water heater as the tornado hit. After the storm passed, they went upstairs to find their house and garage completely gone. So was the dog.

Thankfully, the next day, the Dane County Sheriff's

Office found the dog and brought it to a veterinary clinic for minor injuries. The local TV news ran a story on the dog to try to locate its owner. The family was happily reunited.

Everyone had painful stories of courage and survival, and they found comfort knowing they could get through it all together.

The Stoughton tornado was one of twenty-seven tornadoes that touched down in the state of Wisconsin on August 18, 2005. This tornado was the most treacherous. The tornado was classified as an F3 tornado, which meant its winds were 158 to 206 mph and would cause devastating damage to homes, businesses, and the environment.

The family dog, Madison.

Glass Storm

Steve hammering the building permit into the ground for the Lovell's new home.

Stephen's bucket of salamanders from the window wells.

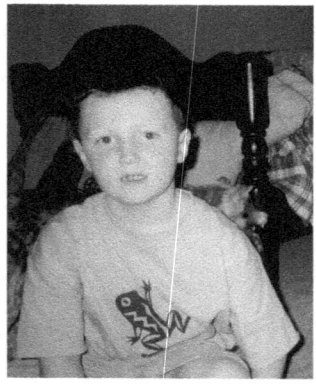

Stephen in his favorite shirt and Madi just checking in.

Mary running through sprinkler.

Glass Storm

The aerial view of the window well and glass block windows, the same ones Sally looked out during the tornado.

Mary observing Stephen in the window well looking for salamanders.

Sally and Mary Lovell

Mary and Madi bundled up during a snow day.

Mary's dance recital costume.

Mary and Molly, her American Girl doll, dressed in Norwegian outfits.

Stephen holding a toad.

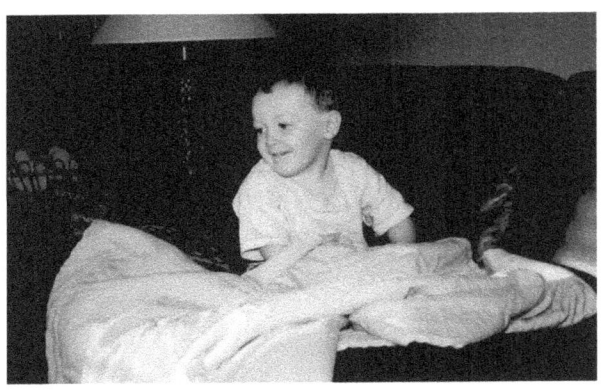
Stephen with 'Blankie'.

Sally and Mary Lovell

The Stoughton Tornado on August 18th, 2005.

Glass Storm

Only the foundation was left.

A smashed, flipped car.

The first scenes Steve, Mary, and Stephen saw coming into Stoughton, WI.

Sally and Mary Lovell

A house leveled in the path of the tornado.

Glass Storm

The calm after the storm.

In the wake of destruction, the tree stood:
a monument to resilience.

Sally and Mary Lovell

Mary and Stephen looking at the beautiful oak tree, years later, at the corner of Sheryl Lane and Linnerud Drive. It survived the storm.

Glass Storm

The carved wooden bear from the Country Club trees.

Sally and Mary Lovell

The Lovell Family.

Glass Storm

The Lovell Family, several years later with Ellie,
their new Teacup Schnauzer.

CHAPTER 10

The Big, Bad Wolf

The drive back from the Days Inn to Stoughton was somber. The Lovells sat in traffic for most of the trip because debris still blocked the roads. The car in front of them had a bumper sticker that read *Tough times don't last, tough people do*.

"I don't know what today is going to be like," Sally told her family. "But I know we're a tough family that can get through anything together."

Steve reached over and squeezed Sally's hand. Mary caught their shared expressions and smiled. She and her brother's lives were forever changed. Yesterday, life had been so carefree. The only decisions they had to make were where to play and what to have for lunch. Madi seemed exhausted still, so Sally held her the entire ride, cradled in her lap.

The Lovells weren't sure exactly what they'd be coming back to, or if they were even going to be allowed back into the house after seeing the damage. They were uncertain of their future and knew they were going to need every ounce of strength for the days ahead.

Before the family could enter the neighborhood, Steve and Sally had to stand in line outside city hall to show their driver's licenses and verify their residency. The family received colored wristbands to wear while inside the disaster area. That week, eight thousand wristbands were assigned to residents, volunteers, and contractors. Officials needed to control the number of people in the area in order to ensure that the affected areas were safe and secure and to limit spectators.

There was so much damage already, the last thing anyone wanted was further harm to their property or loved ones. Officials wanted to ensure there wasn't any looting while relief and cleanup efforts began.

Next, Sally dropped off Madi with a close friend and her family whose nearby home had been spared damage.

Although they were just five minutes away, their home wasn't touched. The Lovells' yard was still unsafe for Madi, and Sally was grateful her friend Sara had offered to watch the dog. Not only that, but she also gave them a change of clothes and shoes. Mary was thankful that she wouldn't have to wear her blue, sparkly flip-flops ever again.

The line of cars waiting to enter the subdivision seemed to stretch for miles as police officers carefully checked each driver for identification. People wanted to share their stories with anyone who'd listen, which also slowed the process.

Finally, the Lovells made it inside. Steve parked the car at the bottom of the hill on Sheryl Lane. There were already enormous piles of rubble collected in the roads near the curb. The Lovells were grateful they had one working car. Some people weren't as fortunate. Sally's car was still inside the marred garage.

The family walked up the hill together, just like the day before. They reached their house and once again stood in the driveway, staring in disbelief.

Sally took Mary and Stephen by the hand and walked to the backyard while Steve went inside to meet with the contractors and insurance agents. The sounds of striking hammers and buzzing chainsaws filled the air. Cleanup had already begun.

Stephen immediately noticed his missing swing set, now lying in a pile on top of the grass that sparkled with shattered glass. It was evident where the set had been because the grass was worn where the swings and slide had stood. Chunks of the ground had been ripped out where the stakes once held the structure in place. The set used to face the big, red barn through the cornfield. After carefully looking at the pieces, Sally figured it had been picked up and dropped because all the nuts and bolts that had held it together were gone.

Stephen never fully understood the extent of what happened during the tornado. Sally had read him the story of *The Three Little Pigs*, and he knew the Big Bad Wolf couldn't blow down the brick house. Therefore, he thought his house also would never be blown down. "Why did the wolf blow my house over, Mom?" he asked.

"Your swing set isn't coming back because of a big storm with lots of wind that blew it over," she patiently tried to explain.

For a moment, he looked at her, perplexed, then asked, "Can we get another one?"

"We can get a new swing set when we get settled into our new house," she said with a smile.

Stephen nodded his approval, smiling for the first time since the tornado. Next, Stephen found eight golf balls perfectly placed in a circle near the swing set. It didn't make sense to anyone. How could they be so carefully placed by such chaotic weather?

Stephen had spent hours playing on the swing set by himself or with friends. It even had a nest, or a play deck, with a green canvas roof and a telescope. Stephen always found a new adventure of how high he could make the swing go or what new way he was going to run up the slide before he slid down. He'd pretend he was Captain Hook trying to spot other ships. He liked to wear a black pirate hat he'd gotten at Disney World when he was younger. In fact, Mary and Stephen had matching pirate hats and liked to pretend they were both pirates fighting over new unexplored territory, also known as the cornfield.

For Mary, the swing set represented freedom. She

always tried to swing as high as the sandhill cranes that visited her yard. Then she'd jump off and land in the soft green grass. Sandhill cranes were native to the area and loved the cornfield and the lake because it provided them food and water. The backyard was the perfect spot for the kids to watch them eat juicy nightcrawlers and corn. The cranes appeared to stand taller than Mary and Stephen, and their red-crested heads and sharp beaks made them so fascinating to observe. They also sang a lovely song when they communicated.

Steve had volunteered to chaperone Mary's class when they took a field trip to the International Crane Foundation in Baraboo, Wisconsin. There, the kids learned about ways to help conserve the crane population. The birds are an endangered species, with some types of cranes making the red list of threatened species. Sally even took continuing education classes at the foundation.

"Oh no! Grandpa and Grandma's apple trees are gone!" Mary suddenly cried.

She ran toward the right side of the yard to examine the gaping holes in the ground. Sure enough, the tornado had uprooted the two apple trees Mary and

Stephen's grandparents had given the kids as a gift when they came to visit. They'd planted the apple trees near the edge of the cornfield next to the strawberry patch Steve had planted for Sally a few years earlier. Grandma and Grandpa had taken the kids outside with a shovel to plant the saplings. They dug two holes a few feet apart, with Grandpa telling the kids to think of them every time new buds sprouted in the spring.

For years, the trees had grown a few shiny, delicious, bright red apples. The kids called their grandparents often as they picked them and proudly took the fruits to school to eat during lunch. In the summers, Mary and Stephen couldn't wait to pick the small but juicy homegrown strawberries. Their fingers and faces would be stained red afterward. Unfortunately, the fragile apple trees and the strawberry patch were no match for the tornado's winds.

CHAPTER 11

Is That Replaceable?

Sally and the kids walked back around to the driveway to see Steve still speaking with the contractors and insurance agent.

"Is it safe for us to come in?" Sally asked the contractor.

"Yes, but don't let the kids wander too far away from you."

The insurance agent then said, "Everyone will have to wear utility gloves who helps on your property. Also, don't wear sandals because of the sharp debris. Glass has been sprayed like sandpaper on everything."

With that knowledge, Sally and the kids walked through the front door, the same door Sally had slammed shut less than a day ago as the tornado barreled down the fairway toward her. Furniture was strewn about and thrown down the hallway into the walls. They stepped lightly on broken glass toward the kitchen. There, three large steak knives had been thrown from the butcher block to pierce the wall in a straight line, just like darts on a dartboard. Dishes were shattered on the floor, and most of the cabinet doors were missing. It already had been decided the roof would be replaced immediately—there were a number of broken rafters, and they didn't want it to collapse on the rest of the house.

Mary spotted the pan of scotcheroos her mom had been making for the funeral and went to pick it up.

"Stop!" Sally yelled, but it was too late.

Mary cried out and quickly dropped the pan. "Ouch!" Shards of glass were sticking out of the dessert and its disposable pan. Mary's hands began gushing blood. "When am I going to stop getting hurt from this tornado?"

Sally found a roll of paper towels and bottled water to clean Mary's hands. "It's just temporary," she said soothingly. "These wounds will heal."

The damage to their home was almost unbearable. It

defied logic. The tornado had flattened homes, cars, and landscapes, but Stephen's thumbprint angel still hung peacefully untouched on the broken light fixture. Sally was once again reminded how incredibly fortunate she was to escape the storm unscathed.

To the left of the kitchen was the toy room, which once so neatly held the kids' computer, bookshelves, toys, and a large sofa. Sally had already purchased their back-to-school items. Backpacks, lunchboxes, pens, pencils, markers, crayons, glue, folders, notebooks, and scissors had been carefully arranged inside. Everything had vanished.

"How am I going to go to school if I don't have my supplies?" Stephen asked, concerned. No one answered.

One window scarcely held the remains of the wooden blinds that had once blocked views of such scary storms. The shiny metal box brackets and screws hung exposed on the inside of the wooden frame. Stephen had recently celebrated his seventh birthday and now had lost all the toys and games he'd received at his frog and salamander party. The Harry Potter and Hogwarts Castle Lego set and make-believe zoo he'd created in the corner of the room also had been blown away. He'd spent countless hours making sure each animal was in the correct stall.

"How am I going to have friends over if I don't have toys to share with them?" Stephen asked. To him, there was nothing better than his toys. Again, no one knew what to say.

Sally and the children made their way down the hallway and upstairs to their bedrooms. At first, they were hesitant because they didn't know how sturdy the support beams were after the nearly 200-mph winds. However, with the contractor's approval, they forged on.

At the top of the steps was the large, now-blown-out arched picture window that overlooked the golf course. It offered their first in-person aerial view of their neighborhood. They could trace the path of the tornado through the once perfectly straight rows of corn, now matted with layers of debris that pointed east. Mother Nature had shown little mercy.

Sally, Mary, and Stephen continued down the hallway to their bedrooms and stared at a large, solid-oak door that lay sideways on the floor. It had to weigh at least fifty pounds.

"Mom, I don't think that door is supposed to be in the middle of the hallway," Mary said.

"Just keep walking," Sally said. "I'm sure we'll find where it came from soon enough."

Stephen's room was on the left and had a life-sized mural painted like the book *The Salamander Room*. Frogs and salamanders climbed up the walls on giant green leaves and brown vines that hung from trees. Their incredible friend Sara, who had Madi, had painted murals in both the kids' bedrooms.

As they entered, they saw Stephen's twin bed, with its red, blue, and green plaid bedding, pushed up against the corner of the room. Yet Blankie, his baby blanket, and Trumpy, his stuffed elephant, lay in the middle of the bed, accounted for.

A yellow rolling suitcase full of marbles had been sliced open, and hundreds of shiny, multicolored glass marbles littered the carpet. A red backpack full of Power Rangers had been slammed into a wall—there was a red mark where it had hit and dropped to the floor.

Stephen was grateful nothing had happened to Blankie and Trumpy, but the remainder of his childhood toys were lost in the storm. He knew he wasn't responsible for the tornado, but he felt he was being punished. A moose night-light that had stood atop his nightstand was on the floor. Strips of broken wood shaped like serrated knives and pieces of insulation that looked like cotton candy littered his carpet. Not a single article of clothing remained that wasn't covered with shards of broken glass.

Mary knew her room would be inspected next, and a feeling of dread came over her. She walked the few steps from Stephen's room to find both of her bedroom windows gone. Curtains swayed in and out of the frames.

"What would have happened if the tornado had come later last night while I was fast asleep?" Mary asked.

More questions that Sally didn't know how to answer. How could she comfort her kids after the worst had happened? Instead, she just held her daughter tightly as they slowly made their way inside the room. The left side of Mary's room had a fairytale mural of a white picket fence that extended the length of the entire wall. Pink hollyhocks stretched halfway to the ceiling. Sally's mom had grown up with the same flowers flanking her childhood cottage like guardsmen. In the center of the fence stood an eight-foot-tall, weather-beaten arched trellis. Green ivy encompassed the entire trellis, and tiny, blue morning glories—Mary's favorite flowers—delicately dotted the green vines.

Mary's most loved gray-and-white-striped stuffed cat named Abby sat in the corner of the fence with its tail wrapped around a post. Abby wore a sparkly pink collar and a tag with her name etched in silver. Now the once magical mural was distorted, missing large chunks of plaster across its entirety where objects had pelted the wall.

All that was left of the sheer white, sparkly canopy that had hung elegantly from the ceiling over Mary's bed were the holes where it had been attached. Broken glass, torn corn husks, and yellow insulation covered the gray carpeting. Her bed and dresser had shifted toward the windows but hadn't quite made it out of the room. Mary was most upset because only bits and pieces remained of her collections of American Girl, Polly Pockets, and Barbie dolls. Most of the dolls she'd never see again. Her clothes also had shards of glass sliced through them and were strewn around her room. Losing her dance costumes troubled her—she knew she'd never get another pink-and-white, sparkly tutu from her dance recital.

Looking again at Mary's bedroom furniture, Sally felt her stomach fall. She shuddered, imagining Mary sleeping in her bed, getting sucked out of the window and up into the tornado. Mary certainly weighed much less than her heavy bedroom furniture, and that had just about been sucked out. She had come so close to losing her daughter forever.

As they neared Sally and Steve's bedroom, it became clear that the solid oak door in the hallway had come from inside. The powerful winds had ripped the door off its hinges and thrown it down the hall. Inside, their four-poster bed was still intact, but pieces of shingles were lodged into the sides of the bed. The cream-colored carpet was covered with leaves, shingles, cornstalks, bricks, and sharp pieces of wood. The TV was smashed on the floor, and the sweater chest had pieces of glass and deep gashes. It wasn't surprising the windows were blown out here as well.

"Oh, no!" Sally frantically screamed, combing the room with her eyes.

The kids followed her but didn't know what was wrong. Sally had been baking and cleaning the house when the tornado hit, so she'd taken off her wedding ring so it wouldn't be in the way. She'd placed it on the Waterford Crystal ring stand that she kept on her nightstand. Her mother had given it to her shortly after Steve proposed. Neither the stand nor the ring was anywhere to be found. Sally assumed they'd been sucked out the window.

"What's wrong?" Steve called as he ran up the stairs and down the hallway.

Sally ran over and threw her arms around him and told him what had happened. "I'm so sorry! I never meant for this to happen! I'm just so, so sorry. Please don't be mad!"

"Rings are replaceable," Steve said as he held Sally in his arms, trying to console her. "*You* are not."

CHAPTER 12

Here Comes the Family

The repetitive sounds of chainsaws, bulldozers, and generators filled the air. The grinding, beeps, and crashes lasted for days. Power remained out, so an impressive number of American Red Cross and Salvation Army volunteers worked to set up meal stations for residents. There also wasn't running water because of all the damaged pipes, so cooking wasn't a feasible option.

Lines of people waiting for the porta potties stretched along the neighborhood streets, having to occasionally step aside to make way for the four-wheelers who were delivering water. Saint Ann's, Mary and Stephen's school and the parish in which Mary had received her baptismal and first communion sacraments, was already set up to cook and serve meals to the victims. In fact, this was made possible because Steve's brother-in-law donated over 3,000 pounds of meat—ground beef, roast beef, and deli meats—to the church and victims.

Cleanup crews donated thousands of hours to ensure life would return to a new normal in Stoughton.

Hand-in-hand, the Lovells walked down Sheryl Lane to a giant tent set up with food. There aren't words for how grateful they were for the volunteers who were helping them at their most critical moments. Residents sat at long, white folding tables with brown, metal folding chairs, already set up for the hundreds of victims and volunteers who needed to be fed.

The arrangement looked eerily familiar to Mary. "Mom? Dad? Is it possible that these are the exact tables where we ate cookies yesterday? They look familiar."

After the family ate lunch, Steve's phone rang. Relatives were waiting for wristbands at the entrance to the neighborhood. Steve decided it was a good time for a walk to clear his head from all the turmoil. Family members were arriving from Illinois, Iowa, and neighboring Wisconsin towns to help in any way and be supportive. They came with heavy boots and utility gloves, plastic bags, boxes, and an array of tools. They even brought coolers of food and drinks and ice cream pails full of cookies.

Steve's sister-in-law hung a paper sign on the front door that read *God Bless This Mess*. He broke down and cried at the outpouring of love, support, and generosity from his family.

Steve hadn't gone into his office yet and was grateful to have his brothers and sisters there to console him—his family's livelihood depended on what remained in the room. Steve finally walked inside and stared in shock. His once perfectly organized office was destroyed. It looked like a war zone. He told his family he needed help cleaning and packing up the office. "We'll need a shovel and wheelbarrow to clean this up," he said.

The strong winds had made this room like a dumping ground. A wooden filing cabinet that weighed around eight hundred pounds lay on the floor on its side. Both large windows had been blown out. An array of garbage, including shingles, tools, rakes, corn husks, shoes, and shredded tree limbs, engulfed the green, speckled carpet.

Containers of paint and cleaners lay in puddles that were staining the carpeting. They'd need a shovel to pick up all the glass that was embedded in the walls. The sound of broken glass being shoveled and poured into rubber garbage cans would be embedded in the minds of the entire family for years to come.

Sally's family drove down from her hometown in Upper Michigan with a donated pickup truck and trailer to help haul away debris and also to pack up salvaged possessions to move the Lovells north to their new location in Menominee with Sally's parents. Sally's brother and his wife were in the process of adopting a child, so Sally was grateful they took the time to help her when they had other priorities at home. Mary and Stephen were excited to learn they'd soon have a new baby cousin. In such a devastating time, it brought a hopeful new beginning to Sally's entire family.

Their aunts and uncles made sure Mary and Stephen had company the entire time they were there. Sally's motherly instincts kicked in when she noticed Stephen was becoming overwhelmed by the number of people around their house. He became quiet and withdrawn.

"Can you please take Stephen for a walk to the oak tree?" Sally asked her sister.

Stephen started on the walk with his aunt, clutching a net in one hand in case he spotted an amphibian in need of rescue. They walked up Sheryl Lane to the oak tree and turned right on Linnerud Drive to see more damage. Most of the houses were flattened.

A neighbor was searching through debris, trying to salvage anything he could. There was a car jammed into a living room fireplace. The car didn't belong to that household, but instead to the house about thirty yards down the street. It was almost incomprehensible that a car could be moved down the street and end up in a neighbor's living room. But then again, entire neighborhoods had been flattened. It had started to feel as though there wasn't anything the tornado hadn't touched.

They soon ended up waiting in line at the blue porta potty. The weather was scorching for Wisconsin, with temperatures reaching the upper eighties and high humidity levels. While waiting in line, Stephen and his aunt heard more stories of survival. One that stuck out was about the same family that lost its whole house. The boy was a huge fan who'd lost all of his University of Wisconsin-Madison and Green Bay Packers football gear, so he was invited to meet the entire UW-Madison Badgers football team. During the game that followed, he also received Packers tickets and memorabilia—another incredible example of how the community joined together to help someone during the frightful time.

After what seemed like hours, it was Stephen's turn to use the porta potty. He was reluctant because it was his first time using one. Thirty minutes later, his aunt was apologizing to everyone in line for how long her nephew was taking.

"Stephen? Are you okay in there?"

Finally, Stephen emerged. "Thanks for waiting," he told everyone in a sweet voice. "I enjoyed the quiet time."

CHAPTER 13

Losses and Gains

While Sally packed what dishes hadn't been smashed, Mary donned utility gloves, getting right in on the action by using a snow shovel to move pound upon pound of broken glass and debris.

Mary then used an old broom and dustpan to clean up what she could. Frustration crept up on her, and she made several attempts to get the glass to come up from the carpeting. She kept trying and trying until finally, she began to cry. "This isn't fair that God let a tornado break my house for no reason," she told her mother, tears streaming down her face.

Sally held her tightly. "Everything is going to be

okay," she said. "The sadness you're feeling right now is temporary, I promise."

Sally took the broom from Mary's hands and suggested that she take a break in her room.

Just then, the phone rang. The family's insurance agent was calling to tell them to stop cleaning—their coverage would pick up the cost of professional cleanup and removal.

It wasn't long before cleanup and restoration companies arrived. Working efficiently, and with time and care, these companies helped the Lovells preserve some of their belongings. Lost and Found tables were set up around the city and at Stoughton High School so people could search for missing items.

Mail service was canceled for many weeks, and Sally had to go get the mail from a lockbox at the downtown post office. Pieces of mail had been blown all around neighboring Wisconsin cities and were kindly sent back to their owners in Stoughton for weeks and months after the tornado hit.

Sally and Mary Lovell

~ ~ ~

Mary walked up the stairs and down the hall to her room. It was dark inside because someone had boarded up the windows with plywood. She couldn't look out at the cornfield to see the birds flying like she had since she was a baby. Debris still covered her floor. She sat on a plastic chair and ate a ham sandwich alone in her once beautiful, princess-inspired room.

Mary's tears were interrupted by a knock on her door, a sign that her friend had come to help her pack up her room. Even at just nine years old, Mary wanted to seem stronger than she was. She thought about how she had just days to say goodbye to the only life she'd known, the lump in her throat refusing to budge.

"Thanks for being my friend right now," Mary said, hugging her friend tightly. "I really need it."

The lump in her throat turned into tears, and this time Mary didn't want to be strong. She was hurting, and she didn't care who knew it. She was scared of moving to a new house and making new friends at a new school. Mary didn't understand her parents' decision to move, but she did understand why her mom wanted to be close to her family. Her mom just came face-to-face with death, and Sally wanted to be with her mom and dad.

Sally didn't know it then, but she'd have nightmares for years about opening her front door and seeing a spiraling wind vortex. Her world had been tipped upside down in the blink of an eye.

Mary was at an age where she understood what she'd lost, but also what she could gain from the tragedy. She was always the type of child who wanted to do something kind and be helpful to others.

Before the tornado, she made sure she put money in the collection basket at church, took donations to the food pantry, passed out May Day baskets of candy to the neighbors, and sold a massive amount of Girl Scout cookies. She prepared months ahead of time for her school's talent show, where she proudly played the piano and danced to the Cheetah Girls and Bryan Adams. She always had a large group of friends, but was content being alone and reading, knitting, sewing, cooking, or practicing yoga.

When the tornado hit, she lost nearly everything she

owned. For a nine-year-old, that can cause considerable trauma. But instead, Mary saw a community she'd known her whole life come together and help her in ways she hadn't known were possible. She witnessed the heart and soul of what a true community meant. Strangers came to her house and offered to help her dig through debris. Volunteers provided valuable services and fed her and her family for days.

Near and dear family and friends sat with her and played games while her parents worked with contractors and the insurance company. Those same friends showed up every day and hauled debris to the curb, sorting and packing up items that were salvageable. It was unbelievable how generous they were with their time.

Before the kids left, they placed a statue of St. Joseph inside a clear bag and sealed it. While his family watched, Steve buried it facing the house. He placed it next to the window well where Stephen caught salamanders. Supposedly it would help the house sell more quickly.

Sally's brother and sister-in-law were gracious enough to drive down again from Menominee so they could pick up Mary, Stephen, and Madi and move them into their grandparents' house. Sally and Steve would come up a few days later to enroll the kids in their new school and get them settled while they stayed in their Madison hotel to figure out the details of contractors and insurance. Steve and Sally slept better once their children were removed from the chaotic environment.

The kids suffered severe night terrors for months. They desperately missed their home, parents, and friends. Sally's parents showered them with unconditional love and compassion and became their foundation to their new surroundings. Mary and Stephen didn't have many clothes left, and their new school required uniforms. Grandma and Grandpa took them to Kmart to buy new shoes, pajamas, and school supplies.

Sally's parents did their best to ensure the transition went as smoothly as possible. They knew Steve and Sally had enough turmoil to deal with in Stoughton. For a few days, Grandma, Grandpa, and Sally's sister and brother-in-law took Mary and Stephen to their cottage on the lake in Upper Michigan. The kids had spent many summers with cousins at the cottage. They built sandcastles, ate hamburgers and s'mores for dinner, and even watched cartoons before bed. For a short time, they were able to feel the familiar, peaceful feeling that only family can bring.

CHAPTER 14

New Beginnings

The day finally came the following summer when Steve and Sally met with the real estate agent to sell their home. The entire community had come together to help the Lovells and all their neighbors—moving to a new city wouldn't be easy. Strangers had donated their time, food, money, and talents, but most importantly, had given comfort and care to the Stoughton community during a difficult time. These great people stayed with the families until the last box was packed or thrown out.

Steve and Sally planned to stop at their home one last time before they made their way to the closing. It was going to be a day of closure because it was time to dig up the St. Joseph statue and bring it to their new house.

As they drove back along their old road, the sounds of drills and hammers still echoed, hard at work, over a year later. Some houses that had been demolished were back as though nothing had happened. Stakes held up newly planted saplings, and new driveways were being poured. Brightly colored American flags once again waved proudly on houses.

"Do you remember the lemonade stands the kids had at the bottom of the driveway?" Sally asked as they pulled up to their house.

"Of course. Hopefully they'll have lemonade stands at our new house, too."

Steve parked in front of the new white garage doors. They looked so different, no longer sucked in toward the house. It felt strange to Steve not to pull into the garage, but he quickly reminded himself it no longer was his garage.

The couple walked around the edge of the yard and reminisced about all the good times they'd shared there. They remembered how the kids ran through the sprinkler in their bare feet on warm summer days, Madi barking with excitement. They stopped and stared where the swing set had stood. They walked where the strawberry patch and the apple trees had been. Steve recalled hiring a company to "vacuum" the grass with a special machine equipped to suck up glass and debris after the storm. However, glass still remained, so new sod was placed. The grass now looked like plush, green carpeting.

A tear trickled from the corner of Sally's eye and ran down her cheek. Steve stopped to wipe her face and squeezed her hand tighter.

"Hey, Sal?" Steve said. "We're a family no matter where we are, remember? It has got nothing to do with the house itself—it's our love that makes it a home."

They made their way to the other side of the house and smiled at how Sally's beautiful white hydrangeas had returned, bigger than ever. Then they looked down to the bottom of the hill. Lake Kegonsa was full of boaters on a hot summer day.

Sally was reminded of all the times she ran up and down the hill in her triathlon training. "Remember when I broke my foot running here?"

Steve nodded. "You thought you were invincible and continued to run!"

Back in front of the house again, Steve opened the door for Sally. The scent of fresh paint and new carpet filled the air. Today, they'd remove their shoes so they didn't mark the newly refinished flooring. The warm wood tones of the floor no longer bore the scars from unidentified objects that had so uninvitingly ripped into its flesh. When they entered the kitchen, the cabinets and appliances were gleaming as the sun shone through the windowpanes. Even the countertops were free of any sign of the storm.

Sally looked up at the new light fixture that hung where the kitchen table and thumbprint angel once were. She marveled once again at how the angel had survived unscathed. In fact, for their next anniversary, Steve mounted the angel in a shadow box and presented it to Sally. It now hangs on a wall near the door of their new home as a reminder of life's perseverance from August 18, 2005.

Steve and Sally then walked down the basement steps and silently stood in the bathroom where Sally and Madi had taken shelter from the storm. They didn't need to say anything. They both knew it could have been the place Steve and the kids had found Sally and Madi lifeless.

So much had happened since the night of the tornado. Sally wasn't the same person—her life had a new purpose and meaning after coming face-to-face with death. Still haunted by extremely realistic nightmares, it was clear that although she had only looked at the tornado for a few seconds, it had made a lifelong impact. For Sally, life became more about living in the moment. Whenever she made scotcheroos, she always made sure Stephen and Mary got the first bite. Her life became more about hugging her children a little more tightly each night at bed, and more about being sure to mark each day by expressing her love for her entire family.

These changes helped her fight back against that wicked tornado in the best way she could: with love. Sally and Steve had so many bittersweet memories tugging at their heartstrings as they locked the front door and drove away for the last time. How were they supposed to feel? Sally felt a piece of the house would always live inside of her. The couple knew they'd miss their home, their neighborhood, and all the wonderful friends they had there.

But Steve reminded Sally, "It's time for the next chapter of our life to begin."

CHAPTER 15

Bent, But Not Broken

On Mary and Stephen's first day of school in Upper Michigan, Grandma walked them both to their classrooms and explained to their teachers that she was going to be "Mom" for a few weeks. Their new classmates welcomed them by making heartfelt cards and giving Mary a stuffed dog and Stephen a stuffed bear because they knew they had lost their toys in the tornado.

Mary turned ten a few months later. In lieu of gifts, she asked her new friends to donate to the local animal shelter and enclosed a wish list with the party invitation. The shelter was grateful for Mary's generosity. Her parents knew she was reacting to what she'd witnessed from the kindhearted people she grew to know after the tornado.

The volunteers and support she witnessed changed her life, and she developed a strong sense of passing it forward. Mary continued the tradition as she grew older and asked that all the presents be donated to a local women's domestic abuse shelter and the American Red Cross. She wanted to make an impact on the world around her, even though she was young. Mary also joined ballet, tap, and jazz dance classes at a studio down the street from her new house, right across the street from Grandpa's old automotive shop.

Stephen also adapted to his new surroundings. He joined a hockey team at a local rink with his cousin. Sally's dad owned a hockey shop that manufactured sports apparel, including hockey jerseys and socks, so Stephen proudly wore his grandfather's equipment to every practice. He was given the opportunity to go to Kmart to purchase several new toys to replace those lost in the tornado. He spent about an hour perusing each aisle. It was comical to watch him pick out the "right" toys. Ironically, even with the chance to replace his belongings with so many new toys, he settled on just two: a pack of Pokémon cards and a new Lego set. It was a proud parent moment. Even at the age of seven, Stephen had learned a valuable life lesson. His experience with the tornado made him realize it was the quality of possessions he had, not the quantity of toys he lost and could've gotten back. Instead, he was just happy to be with his mom.

Madi had the run of the new house. She adapted well and preferred to sleep in Sally's room most nights. She still enjoyed the kids' bedtime rituals, such as taking baths, brushing teeth, and reading books. Her favorite pastime was sitting on the back steps, watching the peaceful waves wash up on the shores of Green Bay. Madi deserved to live the rest of her life like that. She was a blessing, and the Lovells were forever grateful for her.

When the family began unpacking boxes of old belongings, Sally was hesitant for fear that broken glass would show up. Sure enough, inside the first box she opened, she found a small blue keepsake box. Inside were four pieces of glass and part of a shingle.

The Stoughton tornado showed the power of resiliency and regeneration. A year after the storm, a gathering took place at the oak tree on the end of Sheryl Lane and Linnerud Drive. That big, old, beautiful tree was bent, but not broken, during the storm and now stood mighty and tall as ever. One of the trees destroyed on the fairway of the country club was carved into a bear statue by an artist. It was incredible to see it turned into something so perfectly crafted.

In its "Stoughton Area Tornado After Action Report," the Dane County Department of Emergency Management said the tornado caused seventeen miles of damage. It destroyed sixty-nine homes, severely damaged eighty-four more, and caused minor issues to two hundred other homes. In total, the tornado caused nearly $34 million in damage and claimed two lives. A total of 3,590 volunteers and officials helped rebuild the community, including EMS crews, hospital workers, firefighters, law enforcement officers, and humane services crews. A combined 38,000 hours and 52,000 meals were provided by the Salvation Army and the American Red Cross, and $320,000 was donated from various organizations. Because of all the damage to the farms and businesses in the area, the US Department of Agriculture helped farmers with equipment and crop reconstruction, and the US Small Business Administration helped assist businesses and homeowners.

The Lovell family was humbled by the kindness shown by the community, volunteers, and their family and friends. For years, they'd watched commercials on weather-related tragedies and news coverage of the devastation. Now the Lovells had witnessed firsthand how volunteer groups like the Salvation Army and the American Red Cross and local organizations, schools, clubs, churches, and businesses came directly to them and their neighbors. The volunteers helped rebuild so many lives. The feeling of being part of such a community was immeasurable.

The Lovells adjusted to their new normal, but they never stopped appreciating the extraordinary examples of sacrifice and the long hours the entire community put into making sure a smile was on everyone's face. They found strength they never knew they had. It was stressful for all because the glass storm was out of their control. However, despite the twister's massive destruction and all the people and pets affected, this natural disaster brought out the best qualities of humanity. After all, Stephen's thumbprint angel didn't surrender just because the wind blew.

Glass Storm

The thumb print angel that survived the tornado, untouched.

Sally's Scotcheroo Recipe

Ingredients:

1 cup light corn syrup
1 cup white sugar
2 cups peanut butter
7 cups crisped rice cereal
2 cups chocolate chips
2 cups butterscotch chips

Instructions:

Microwave corn syrup in a microwave safe bowl until melted. Add peanut butter and stir until mixed. Add cereal to mixing bowl, and pour corn syrup/peanut mixture over it. Stir. Pour into a greased 9 x 13 pan and smooth. Melt chocolate chips and butterscotch chips together, and pour over the cooled cereal mixture. Cool and cut into bars.

Mary's Tornado Survival Kit

Large Tupperware container
First-aid kit
Bottled water
Granola bars
Flashlight with batteries
Blankets
Coloring books and crayons
Extra shoes
Dog food

Reading Guide

Mary made a survival kit long before the tornado hit her house. What items did she include in the kit? Do you agree with her choices? Have you made a survival kit? What items did you include? Why?

Describe a time you or someone you know was in a storm or catastrophic event—a tornado, blizzard, hurricane, earthquake, etc. Where were you? What time of year was it? Were you prepared?

What kind of relationship did Sally and Madi have? Dogs can be trained to detect bombs, drugs, etc. Do you believe Madi sensed the storm was coming? Why? Have you ever experienced a special relationship with an animal?

Mary was asked to be "strong" by her father shortly after the tornado hit. What did he mean by this? Discuss a time when you had to be strong.

Discuss the role the American Red Cross played in the disaster. From Steve taking Mary and Stephen to donate blood to the Red Cross helping the entire Stoughton community recover from the tornado, the agency helped in many ways. How did this inspire Mary to give back?

Despite the sadness of the disaster, how did the Lovell family overcome the storm's effect and stay positive? How did this experience impact each family member moving forward?

Stephen is overcome with emotion several times in the story. Discuss how showing emotion is beneficial to recovery. How did Stephen cope with losing his toys? He received the opportunity to replenish his toys and possessions. What did he choose? Why is this important?

Discuss how the authors use details to describe the events of the tornado. Which event stuck out to you the most? Why?

About the Authors

Sally Lovell has worked in the field of education for more than 30 years. She has taught and tutored at the elementary, middle and high school level. Sally holds a Master of Education degree from Carroll University, Waukesha, Wisconsin, and is a member of the Society of Children's Book Writers & Illustrators, the Wisconsin Writers Association, and Write On, Door County, Fish Creek, Wisconsin. She lives in Green Bay, Wisconsin, with her husband, Steve, and her very spoiled Teacup Schnauzer, Ellie.

Mary Lovell graduated cum laude from the University of Wisconsin-Green Bay in 2017 with a Bachelor of Science degree in human biology and human development. She attends Marquette University School of Dentistry. Mary volunteers her time at area shelters and dental clinics. She is a member of the Society of Children's Book Writers & Illustrators, the Wisconsin Writers Association, and Write On, Door County, Fish Creek, Wisconsin. In her free time, she enjoys traveling with family, scuba diving, kayaking, yoga, knitting, and baking.

www.ingramcontent.com/pod-product-compliance
Lightning Source LLC
Chambersburg PA
CBHW020942090426
42736CB00010B/1227